EKG TEST PREP

EKG Technician Exam Practice Test Questions

Jane John-Nwankwo RN, MSN

EKG TEST PREP: EKG Technician Exam Practice Test Questions

Copyright © 2013 by Jane John-Nwankwo RN, MSN

All rights reserved. No part of this book may be reproduced or transmitted in any form or by any means without written permission from the author.

ISBN-13: 978-1482512748

ISBN-10: 1482512742

Printed in the United States of America.

Dedication

Dedicated to my second daughter Joy, who brought distractions during the compilation of this book but when I looked into her 24-month old face, her innocent smile gave me inspiration to continue.

TABLE OF CONTENTS

Section One..5

Section Two 27

Section Three..49

Section Four..56

Section Five...87

Section Six..103

SECTION ONE QUESTIONS

1. The heart is located in the chest
   A. In front of the sternum in the mediastinal cavity
   B. In the back of the spine between the lungs
   C. Behind the sternum in the mediastinal cavity
   D. Behind the sternum and in the back of the spine

2. The bottom of the heart tilts
   A. Backwards and down, towards the right side of the body
   B. Forwards and down, towards the left side of the body
   C. Backwards and down, towards the left side of the body
   D. Forwards and down, towards the right side of the body

3. The outer layer of the heart is called
   A. Myocardium
   B. Endocardium
   C. Atria

D. Epicardium
4. What surrounds the heart and acts as a tough, protective sac
    A. Pericardium
    B. Myocardium
    C. Epicardium
    D. Endocardium
5. The left atrium receives oxygenated blood through
    A. Pulmonary veins
    B. The inferior and superior vena cavae
    C. Epicardium
    D. Parietal layer
6. The right ventricle receives blood from the right atrium and pumps in through
    A. The pulmonary veins
    B. The aorta
    C. Myocardium
    D. The pulmonary arteries
7. How many valves does the heart contain
    A. 3
    B. 2
    C. 4
    D. 5
8. What are the two AV valves called
    A. Tricuspid and mitral
    B. Left atrium and left ventricle

C. Pulmonic valve and aortic valve
D. Superior vena cava and inferior vena cava

9. What are the semilunar valves called
   A. Right atrium and right ventricle
   B. Pulmonic valve and aortic valve
   C. Tricuspid and mitral valve
   D. Superior vena cava and inferior vena cava

10. What is the coronary ostium?
    A. An opening in the aorta that feeds oxygen to the coronary arteries
    B. A closing in the aorta that feeds blood to the coronary arteries
    C. A closing in the aorta that feeds oxygen to the coronary arteries
    D. An opening in the aorta that feeds blood to the coronary arteries

11. What happens during diastole
    A. Left atrium is filling up with blood, and aortic valve is closed
    B. Left ventricle is filling up with the blood, and aortic valve is closed
    C. Left ventricle is filling up with blood, and aortic valve is open
    D. Left atrium is filling up with bloods, and aortic valve is open

12. The heart is supplied by what two branches of the autonomic nervous system
    A. Norepinephrine and epinephrine
    B. Tricuspid and Mitral
    C. Adrenergic and cholinergic
    D. Atrium and ventricle
13. What are the four characteristics of cardiac cells
    A. Automaticity, excitability, conductivity, and controllability
    B. Conductivity, transitivity, automaticity, and excitability
    C. Excitability, conductivity, automaticity, contractility
    D. Contractility, automaticity, transitivity, and excitability
14. The ability of a cell to transmit an electrical impulse to another cardiac cell is
    A. Automaticity
    B. Conductivity
    C. Excitability
    D. Contractility
15. When a cell is fully depolarized and attempts to return to its resting state is called
    A. Depolarization
    B. Polarized
    C. Repolarization

D. Excitability
16. How many impulses does the SA node generates per minute
    A. 30-40
    B. 40-60
    C. 60-100
    D. 100-200
17. What pacemaker has a firing rate of 40-60 times per minute
    A. Purkinje Fibers
    B. SA node
    C. Bundle of his
    D. AV node
18. The stroke volume is
    A. The amount of blood the heart pumps per minute
    B. The amount of pressure the left ventricle must work against to pump blood into the aorta
    C. The amount of blood ejected with each ventricular contraction
    D. The ability of the heart muscle cells to contract after depolarization
19. What does a lead provide
    A. A view of the heart's electrical activity between two positives poles

    B. A view of the heart's electrical activity between one positive pole and negative pole
    C. A view of the heart's electrical activity between two negative poles
    D. A view of the heart's electrical activity between two positives and two negatives
20. When there's no electrical activity occurring or electrical activity is too weak to measure is called
    A. Isoelectric waveform
    B. Lead
    C. Plane
    D. Interval
21. What refers to a cross-sectional perspective of the heart's electrical activity
    A. Lead
    B. Waveform
    C. Plane
    D. Complex
22. How many types of ECG recording are there
    A. 1
    B. 2
    C. 3
    D. 4

23. This records information from 12 different views of the heart and provides a complete picture of the electrical activity
    A. Rhythm Strip
    B. 12-lead ECG
    C. V leads
    D. Six precordial lead
24. What provides information about the heart's frontal(vertical) plane
    A. 12-lead
    B. Sic precordial lead
    C. Rhythm strip
    D. Six limb leads
25. This provides a continuous cardiac rhythm display and transmits the ECG tracings
    A. Monitor
    B. Lead
    C. Complex
    D. Electrode
26. All bipolar leads have a third electrode called
    A. Lead V1
    B. Lead II
    C. Ground
    D. Cable
27. What lead produces a positive deflection
    A. Lead I
    B. Lead II

C. Lead V2
D. Lead V1

28. In lead aVr where is the positive electrode placed
    A. Left arm
    B. Right foot
    C. Right arm
    D. Left foot

29. Where is lead V1 placed
    A. At the left of the sternum at the fourth intercostal rib space
    B. On the right side of the sternum at the fourth intercostal rib place
    C. At the fifth intercostal space at the midclavicular line
    D. At the right of the sternum at the fifth intercostal rib space

30. Where is lead V5 placed
    A. On the right side of the sternum at the fourth intercostal rib place
    B. Placed at the fifth intercostal space at the anterior axillary line
    C. At the fifth intercostal space at the midclavicular line
    D. At the left of the sternum at the fourth intercostal rib space

31. On a horizontal axis of the ECG strip each small block equals to how many seconds
    A. 0.02
    B. 0.01
    C. 0.40
    D. 0.04

32. When the baseline of the ECG appears wavy, bumpy, or tremulous is called
    A. 60-cycle interference
    B. Waveform interference
    C. Wandering baseline
    D. Electrical interference

33. This is caused by electrical power leakage
    A. Artifact
    B. Waveform interference
    C. 60-cycle interference
    D. Wandering baseline

34. What consists of five waveforms labeled with the letters P,Q,R,S, and T
    A. Interval
    B. Complex
    C. Lead
    D. Artifact

35. What waveform represents atrial depolarization
    A. QRS complex

B. U wave
C. T wave
D. P wave

36. This tracks the atrial impulse from the atria through the AV node, bundle of His, and right and left bundle branches
    A. PR interval
    B. QRS complex
    C. P wave
    D. Q wave

37. This represents the end of ventricular conduction or depolarization and the beginning of ventricular recovery or repolarization
    A. P wave
    B. PR interval
    C. ST segment
    D. QT interval

38. This marks the end of the QRS complex and the beginning of the ST segment
    A. QT interval
    B. PR interval
    C. J point
    D. T wave

39. What waveform represents ventricular recovery or repolarization
    A. P wave
    B. QT interval

C. ST segment
D. T wave

40. This measures ventricular depolarization and repolarization
    A. QT interval
    B. ST segment
    C. P wave
    D. T wave

41. What represents the recovery period of the Purkinje or ventricular conduction fibers
    A. T wave
    B. U wave
    C. QRS complex
    D. ST segment

42. What is the easiest way to calculate heart rate especially if the rhythm is irregular
    A. 1500 method
    B. Sequence method
    C. 10 times method
    D. 5 times method

43. The normal duration of a P wave is
    A. 0.06-0.10
    B. 0.36-0.44
    C. 0.12-0.20
    D. 0.06-0.12

44. The normal duration of a PR interval is
    A. 0.06-0.12

B. 0.12-0.20
  C. 0.36-0.44
  D. 0.06-0.10

45. The normal duration of a QT interval is
  A. 0.12-0.20
  B. 0.06-0.12
  C. 0.36-0.44
  D. 0.06-0.10

46. How many steps are there to interpret a rhythm strip
  A. 10
  B. 8
  C. 6
  D. 5

47. What acts as the heart's primary pacemaker
  A. SA node
  B. AV node
  C. Bundle of His
  D. Purkinje fibers

48. During inspiration, an increase in the flow of blood back to the heart reduces vagal tone, and does what to the heart's heart rate
  A. Increases the heart's rate
  B. Decreases the heart's rate
  C. Stays within normal limit
  D. Decreases and increases the hearts rate

49. This is characterized by a sinus rate below 60 beats/ minute and a regular rhythm
    A. Sinus tachycardia
    B. Sinus Arrhythmia
    C. Sinus bradycardia
    D. Sinus arrest

50. Drugs like beta- adrenergic blockers, Lithium (lithobid), and propafenone (Rhythmol) are used to treat what?
    A. Sinus bradycardia
    B. Sinus arrest
    C. Sinus tachycardia
    D. Sinus arrhythmia

51. When administering atropine, the correct dosage to give is
    A. .05mg
    B. 0.5mg
    C. .3mg
    D. 3mg

52. What is the sinus rate for sinus tachycardia
    A. 60 beats / minute
    B. 40 beats / minute
    C. 120 beats / minute
    D. 80 beats / minute

53. What causes sinus arrest
    A. Lack of electrical activity in the atrium

B. Lack of electrical activity in the ventricles
C. Sinus tachycardia
D. Sinus bradycardia

54. What refers to a wide spectrum of SA node abnormalities
    A. Sinus bradycardia
    B. Sick sinus syndrome
    C. Sinus tachycardia
    D. Sinus arrest

55. What is supplied by blood from the right coronary artery and left circumflex artery
    A. AV node
    B. Purkinje fibers
    C. Bundle of his
    D. SA node

56. During sinus bradycardia what is given for hypotension
    A. Atropine
    B. Epinephrine
    C. Dopamine
    D. Beta- adrenergic blocker

57. What results from a dysfunction of the sinus node's automaticity or abnormal conduction or blockages of impulses coming out of the nodal region
    A. Sinus arrest

      B. Sinus tachycardia
      C. Sinus bradycardia
      D. Sick sinus syndrome

58. What is another word for sick sinus syndrome
      A. Sinus nodal dysfunction
      B. Epinephrine
      C. Sinus arrest
      D. Dopamine

59. What is the most common cardiac rhythm disturbances, results from impulses originating in areas outside the SA node
      A. Premature atrial contractions
      B. Atrial arrhythmias
      C. Atrial fibrillation
      D. Atrial flutter

60. The three mechanisms of atrial arrhythmias are
      A. Circus automaticity, enhanced reentry, afterdepolarization
      B. Afterdepolarization, enhance reentry, circus automaticity
      C. Enhance automaticity, enhance reentry, afterdepolarization
      D. Circus reentry, afterdepolarization, enhance automaticity

61. The ability of cardiac cells to initiate impulses on their own is
      A. Enhance automaticity

    B. Circus reentry
    C. Afterdepolarization
    D. Circus automaticity

62. This originates outside the SA node and usually result from an irritable spot, or focus, in the atria that takes over as pacemaker for one or more beats
    A. AV node
    B. Bundle of His
    C. Premature atrial contractions
    D. Sinus arrhythmias

63. Partial repolarization can lead to a repetitive ectopic firing called
    A. Afterdepolarization
    B. Triggered activity
    C. Enhance automaticity
    D. Reentry

64. When alcohol, nicotine, anxiety, fatigue, fever, and infectious diseases are presence what commonly occurs in a normal heart
    A. Premature atrial contractions
    B. Enhance automaticity
    C. Triggered activity
    D. Circus reentry

65. What has atrial rate from 150 to 250 beats / minute
    A. Atrial bradycardia

B. SA node
C. AV node
D. Atrial tachycardia

66. The three types of atrial tachycardia are
    A. Paroxysmal atrial tachycardia, multifocal atrial tachycardia, atrial bradycardia
    B. Paroxysmal atrial bradycardia, multifocal atrial tachycardia, atrial tachycardia with block
    C. Paroxysmal atrial tachycardia, multifocal atrial bradycardia, atrial tachycardia with block
    D. Paroxysmal atrial tachycardia, multifocal atrial tachycardia, atrial tachycardia with block

67. What is characterized by abnormal p waves that produce a saw-toothed appearance
    A. Atrial fibrillation
    B. Atrial flutter
    C. Bundle of His
    D. Premature atrial contractions

68. This is caused by conditions that enlarge atrial tissues and elevate atrial pressures
    A. Atrial flutter
    B. Atrial fibrillation
    C. Premature atrial contractions

D. Bundle of His
69. This is defined as chaotic, asynchronous, electrical activity in atrial tissues
    A. Atrial flutter
    B. Wandering pacemakers
    C. Sinus arrhythmias
    D. Atrial fibrillation
70. This is an irregular rhythm that results when the heart's pacemaker changes its focus from the SA node to another area above the ventricles
    A. Atrial flutter
    B. Wandering pacemaker
    C. Atrial fibrillation
    D. AV node
71. This is distinguished by the absence of P waves and an irregular ventricle response
    A. Atrial flutter
    B. Sinus tachycardia
    C. Sinus bradycardia
    D. Atrial fibrillation
72. The major goal in treating atrial fibrillation is to
    A. Reduce the ventricular response rate to above 100 beats / minute
    B. Reduce the ventricular response rate to below 100 beats / minute

C. Reduce the atrial response rate below to 100 beats / minute
D. Reduce the atrial response rate above 100 beats / minute

ANSWERS FOR SECTION ONE

1. B
2. B
3. D
4. A
5. A
6. D
7. C
8. A
9. B
10. D
11. C
12. C
13. C
14. B
15. C
16. C
17. D
18. C
19. B
20. A
21. C
22. B
23. B
24. D
25. A

26. C
27. B
28. C
29. B
30. B
31. D
32. B
33. C
34. B
35. D
36. A
37. C
38. C
39. D
40. A
41. B
42. C
43. D
44. B
45. C
46. B
47. A
48. A
49. C
50. A
51. B
52. C

53. A
54. B
55. D
56. C
57. D
58. A
59. B
60. D
61. A
62. C
63. B
64. A
65. D
66. D
67. B
68. A
69. D
70. B
71. D
72. B

SECTION TWO QUESTIONS

1. This originates in the atrioventricular (AV) junction- the area around the AV node and the bundle of His
   A. Junctional arrhythmias
   B. P wave
   C. QRS complex
   D. SA node

2. The AV junction is located in the
   A. Upper part of the left atrium near the bicuspid valve
   B. Lower part of the right atrium near the bicuspid valve
   C. Lower part of the right atrium near the tricuspid valve
   D. Upper part if the left atrium near the tricuspid valve

3. This is typically a congenital rhythm disorder that occurs mainly in young children and in adults ages 20 to 35
   A. Premature atrial contractions
   B. Digoxin toxicity
   C. Wolff-Parkinson-white syndrome
   D. Atrial arrhythmias

4. A beat that occurs before a normal beat and cause an irregular rhythm

A. Premature atrial contraction
   B. Premature junctional contraction
   C. Atrial arrhythmias
   D. AV junction
5. This is a string of beats that occur after a conduction delay from the atria
   A. Premature atrial contraction
   B. Premature junctional contraction
   C. Junctional escape rhythm
   D. Atrial arrhythmias
6. The normal firing rate for cells in the AV junction is
   A. 20 to 40 beats/ minute
   B. 60 to 100 beats / minute
   C. 40 to 60 beats / minute
   D. 100 to 140 beats / minute
7. A patient with a junctional rhythm has a slow, regular pulse rate of
   A. 40 to 60 beats/ minute
   B. 20 to 40 beats / minute
   C. 60 to 100 beats / minute
   D. 100 to 140 beats / minute
8. This is given to increase the heart rate during a junctional escape rhythm
   A. Digoxin
   B. Verapamil
   C. Atropine

D. Potassium
9. This is caused by an irritable focus in the AV junction that speeds up to take over as the heart's pacemaker
    A. Junctional tachycardia
    B. Junctional escape rhythm
    C. Premature Junctional contraction
    D. Accelerated Junctional rhythm
10. This occurs when an irritable focus from the AV junction has enhanced automaticity, overriding the SA node to function as the heart's pacemaker
    A. Junctional tachycardia
    B. Accelerated Junctional rhythm
    C. Premature Junctional contraction
    D. Junctional escape rhythm
11. Atrial flutter, multifocal atrial tachycardia, and junctional tachycardia are examples of what
    A. Junctional escape rhythm
    B. Premature junctional contraction
    C. Accelerated junctional rhythm
    D. Supraventricular tachycardia
12. What has a firing rate of 100 to 200 beats /minute
    A. Junctional tachycardia
    B. Atrial bradycardia
    C. Atrial tachycardia

D. Premature juntional contraction
13. What slows the heart rate for the symptomatic patients
    A. Vagal maneuvers
    B. Atropine
    C. Potassium
    D. Digoxin
14. During junctional tachycardia the P wave is inverted in what leads
    A. Lead I, lead II, and lead III
    B. Lead I, lead II, and aVf
    C. aVl, aVf, and aVr
    D. Lead II, lead III, and aVf
15. This occurs when electrical impulses depolarize the myocardium using a different pathway from normal impulses
    A. Ventricular arrhythmias
    B. Premature ventricular contractions
    C. Idioventricular rhythms
    D. Ventricular tachycardia
16. Ventricular arrhythmias originate in the ventricles below the
    A. SA node
    B. AV node
    C. Bundle of His
    D. Purkinje fibers

17. This is an ectopic beat that may occur in healthy people without causing problems
    A. Idioventricular rhythm
    B. Premature ventricular contraction
    C. Ventricular tachycardia
    D. Ventricular fibrillation
18. On a ECG strip, this looks wide and bizarre and appear as early beats causing atrial and ventricular irregularity
    A. Atrial flutter
    B. Ventricular fibrillation
    C. Atrial fibrillation
    D. Premature ventricular contraction
19. This appears when the interval between two normal sinus beats containing a PVC equals two normal sinus intervals
    A. Asystole
    B. Idioventricular rhythm
    C. Compensatory pause
    D. Ventricular tachycardia
20. PVC's that look alike are called
    A. Segments
    B. Couplet
    C. Uniform
    D. Intervals
21. Two PVCs in a row are called
    A. Intervals

B. Uniform
C. Couplet
D. Segments

22. This acts as safety mechanism to prevent ventricular standstill when no impulses are conducted to the ventricular from above the bundle of His
    A. Ventricular tachycardia
    B. Ventricular fibrillation
    C. Premature ventricular contractions
    D. Idioventricular rhythm

23. During Idioventricular rhythm what acts as the heart's pacemaker to generate electrical impulses
    A. His-Purkinje
    B. AV node
    C. SA node
    D. P wave

24. This is also called the rhythms of last resort
    A. Ventricular tachycardia
    B. Idioventricular rhythm
    C. Ventricular escape beat
    D. Premature ventricular contractions

25. When just one idioventricular beat is generated, it's called
    A. Ventricular fibrillation
    B. Asystole

C. Ventricular escape beat
   D. Accelerated idioventricular rhythm
26. When three or more PVCs occur in a row and the ventricular rate exceeds 100 beats/ minute is called
   A. Ventricular tachycardia
   B. Ventricular fibrillation
   C. Premature ventricular contractions
   D. Ventricular bradycardia
27. This means "twisting about the points" and is a special form of polymorphic ventricular tachycardia
   A. PVCs
   B. Torsades de pointes
   C. QT syndrome
   D. V-Fib
28. A chaotic pattern of electrical activity in the ventricles in which electrical impulses arise from many different foci is called
   A. Asystole
   B. PVC
   C. Idioventricular rhythm
   D. Ventricular fibrillation
29. When the patient is completely unresponsive, with no electrical activity in the heart and no cardiac output, what is it called
   A. CPR

B. ACLS
C. Asystole
D. PVC

30. This results from an interruption in the conduction of impulses between the atria and ventricles
    A. SA node
    B. AV node
    C. AV block
    D. SA block

31. In elderly patients, the AV block may be due to what?
    A. Fibrosis of the conduction system
    B. Digoxin toxicity
    C. Cardiomyopathy
    D. Beta- adrenergic blockers

32. When a transvenous catheter is used to locate the area within the heart that participates in initiating or perpetuating certain tachyarrhythmias is called what
    A. Cardiomyopathy
    B. Radiofrequency ablation
    C. AV blocks
    D. Acute myocarditis

33. This occurs when impulses from the atria are consistently delayed during conduction through the AV node

A. Type 1 second- degree AV block
   B. Type 2 second- degree AV block
   C. Third degree AV block
   D. First degree AV block
34. During first- degree AV block the PR interval will be greater than
   A. 0.06 seconds
   B. 20 seconds
   C. 0.5 seconds
   D. 0.20 seconds
35. This occurs when each successive impulse from the SA node is delayed slightly longer than the previous impulse
   A. Type 1 second- degree AV block
   B. First- degree AV block
   C. Type 2 second- degree AV block
   D. Third degree AV block
36. What is another word for Type 1 second- degree AV block
   A. Mobitz type 2 AV block
   B. First- degree AV block
   C. Mobitz type 1 AV block
   D. Third- degree AV block
37. Coronary artery disease, inferior wall MI, and rheumatic fever causes what type of AV block
   A. First- degree AV block
   B. Third- degree AV block

       C. Type 1 second- degree AV block
       D. Type 2 second- degree AV block
38. This occurs when occasional impulses from the SA node fail to conduct to the ventricles
       A. Type 1 second- degree AV block
       B. Type 2 second- degree AV block
       C. Third- degree AV block
       D. First- degree AV block
39. Another word for third- degree AV block is called
       A. Complete heart block
       B. Premature ventricular contractions
       C. Ventricular escape beat
       D. Idioventricular rhythm
40. When impulses from the atria are completely blocked at the AV node and can't be conducted to the ventricles is called what
       A. SA node
       B. First- degree AV block
       C. Type 1 second- degree AV block
       D. Third- degree AV block
41. When the PR interval gradually gets longer with each beat until P wave fails to conduct to the ventricles is what type of AV block
       A. Type 1 second- degree AV block
       B. First- degree AV block
       C. Type 2 second- degree AV block

D. Third- degree AV block
42. When the atria and ventricles beat independently, each controlled by its own pacemaker is called
    A. Bundle of His
    B. AV dissociation
    C. Ventricular escape beat
    D. Acute myocarditis
43. Type 2 second- degree AV block is also known as
    A. Ventricular escape beat
    B. Mobitz type 1 AV block
    C. Mobitz type 2 AV block
    D. Complete heart block
44. This is an artificial device that electrically stimulates the myocardium to depolarize, which begins to contract
    A. Waveform
    B. Rhythm strip
    C. Radiofrequency ablation
    D. Pacemaker
45. What generates an impulse from a power source and transmitting that impulse to the heart muscle
    A. Pacemaker
    B. Electrodes
    C. Wire

  D. Lead

46. Pacemakers consists of what three components
  A. Waveform, interval, segment
  B. Pulse generating, pacing leads, and electrode tip
  C. Wire, electrode, monitor
  D. Lead, electrode, wire

47. How many years does the lithium batteries in a permanent pacemaker last
  A. 1 years
  B. 5 years
  C. 10 years
  D. 7 years

48. This is about the size of a small of a small radio or a telemetry box and is powered by alkaline batteries
  A. Implanted pacemaker
  B. Permanent pacemaker
  C. Temporary pacemaker
  D. Electrode

49. When electric current moves from the pulse generator through the leadwire to the negative pole is what type of lead
  A. Bipolar lead
  B. Lead III
  C. Lead II

D. Unipolar lead

50. In this system, current flows from the pulse generator through the leadwire to the negative pole at the tip
    A. Bipolar lead
    B. Unipolar lead
    C. Lead II
    D. Lead III

51. This sends information about electrical impulses in the myocardium back to the pulse generator
    A. Electrode
    B. Lead
    C. Wire
    D. Monitor

52. A unipolar lead system is more sensitive to the heart's intrinsic electrical activity than
    A. Pacemakers
    B. Bipolar lead
    C. Lead placement
    D. Biventricular pacemaker

53. What is used to treat chronic heart conditions such as AV block
    A. Temporary pacemaker
    B. Biventricular pacemaker
    C. Permanent pacemaker
    D. Epicardial pacemaker

54. What can also serve as a bridge until a permanent pacemaker is inserted
    A. Epicardial pacemaker
    B. Biventricular pacemaker
    C. Synchronous pacemaker
    D. Temporary pacemaker

55. Transvenous, Epicardial, and transcutaneous are types of what pacemakers
    A. Synchronous pacemaker
    B. Epicardial pacemaker
    C. Permanent pacemaker
    D. Temporary pacemaker

56. When inserting the pacemaker through a vein, such as subclavian or internal jugular vein is what type of pacemaker
    A. Epicardial pacemaker
    B. Permanent pacemaker
    C. Transvenous pacemaker
    D. Transcutaneous pacemaker

57. When the doctor attaches the tips of the leadwires to the surface of the heart and then bring the wires through the chest wall, below the incision is what type of pacemaker
    A. Epicardial pacemaker
    B. Transcutaneous pacemaker
    C. Permanent pacemaker
    D. Transvenous pacemaker

58. During a five-letter coding system, the final letter of the code refers to what
    A. The heart chamber in which the pacemaker senses the intrinsic activity
    B. The pacemaker's programmability
    C. The pacemakers response to a tachyarrhythmia
    D. The pacemaker's response to the intrinsic electrical activity it senses in the atrium and ventricle
59. This is used in the treatment of patients with class III and IV heart failure, with both systolic heart failure and ventricular dysynchrony, whose only alternative is heart transplantation
    A. Radiofrequency ablation
    B. Biventricular pacing
    C. DDD pacemaker
    D. Transcutaneous pacemaker
60. This is used to treat arrhythmias in patients who haven't responded to antiarrhythmic drugs or cardioversion
    A. Biventricular pacemaker
    B. Radiofrequency ablation
    C. AAI pacemaker
    D. VVI pacemaker

61. This affects the movement of ions across the cell membrane and alter the electrophysiology of the cardiac cell
    A. Class IV drug
    B. Antiarrhythmic drugs
    C. Class I drug
    D. Procainamide
62. The classification system divides antiarrhythmic drugs into how many major classes
    A. 5
    B. 3
    C. 4
    D. 7
63. The sodium channel or fast channel is also referred to what phase of the classification system
    A. Phase 4
    B. Phase 1
    C. Phase 0
    D. Phase 3
64. Class III drugs block are called what because they block the movement of potassium during phase 3 of the action potential and prolong repolarization and the refractory period
    A. Channel blockers
    B. Calcium channel blockers
    C. Slow channel

D. Potassium channel blockers
65. This drug blocks the movement of calcium during phase 2 of the action potential
    A. Class IV drug
    B. Class II drug
    C. Class I drug
    D. Class III drug
66. These drugs reduce the excitability of the cardiac cell, have an anticholinergic effect, and decrease cardiac contractility
    A. Calcium channel blockers
    B. Sodium channel blockers
    C. Potassium channel blockers
    D. Slow channel blockers
67. What is used to treat patients with supraventricular and ventricular arrhythmias, such as atrial fibrillation or flutter, paroxysmal supraventricular tachycardia, and premature ventricular contractions
    A. Procainamide
    B. Quinidine
    C. Tocainide
    D. Lidocaine
68. These drugs are effective in suppressing ventricular ectopy but aren't used with supraventricular arrhythmias
    A. Class Ic drug

- B. Class Ia drug
- C. Class Ib drug
- D. Class II drug

69. What is used to suppress life- threatening ventricular arrhythmias such as sustained VT
    - A. Lidocaine
    - B. Propafenone
    - C. Amiodarone
    - D. Tocainide

70. Flecainide is used to treat what in patients without structural heart disease and with life- threatening ventricular arrhythmias
    - A. Paroxysmal atrial fibrillation and flutter
    - B. Supraventricular and ventricular arrhythmias
    - C. Supraventricular arrhythmias
    - D. Ventricular fibrillation and flutter

71. What drug slows conduction in all cardiac tissues
    - A. Propafenone
    - B. Dofetilide
    - C. Ibutilide
    - D. Verapamil

72. What drug is used for the rapid conversions of recent- onset atrial fibrillation or flutter to sinus rhythm

A. Verapamil
B. Diltiazem
C. Ibutilide
D. Adenosine

73. Verapamil is used for paroxysmal supraventricular tachycardia because it effects what
    A. P wave
    B. SA node
    C. QRS complex
    D. AV node

74. This is administered I.V. that also is used to treat angina and hypertension
    A. Verapamil
    B. Diltiazem
    C. Adenosine
    D. Atropine

75. What decreases cardiac cell excitability and conductions, slows conduction through the AV node and prolongs the refractory period
    A. Epinephrine
    B. Magnesium sulfate
    C. Atropine
    D. Digoxin

ANSWERS FOR SECTION TWO

1. A
2. C
3. C
4. B
5. C
6. C
7. A
8. C
9. D
10. A
11. D
12. A
13. C
14. D
15. A
16. C
17. B
18. D
19. C
20. C
21. C
22. D
23. A
24. B
25. C
26. A

27. B
28. D
29. C
30. C
31. A
32. B
33. D
34. D
35. A
36. C
37. C
38. B
39. A
40. D
41. A
42. B
43. C
44. D
45. A
46. B
47. C
48. C
49. D
50. A
51. A
52. B
53. C

54. D
55. D
56. C
57. A
58. C
59. B
60. B
61. B
62. C
63. C
64. D
65. A
66. B
67. B
68. C
69. D
70. A
71. A
72. C
73. D
74. B
75. B

SECTION THREE QUESTIONS

1. This is a diagnostic test that helps identify pathologic conditions, especially angina and acute myocardial infarction
    A. Six limb leads
    B. Lead
    C. Electrode
    D. 12-lead ECG
2. Using a special recorder- transmitter, patients at home can transmit ECG by telephone to a central monitoring center for immediate interpretation, this technique is called
    A. 12-lead ECG
    B. Transtelephonic cardiac monitoring
    C. Wire
    D. Electrode
3. The six limb leads records electrical activity in what part of the heart
    A. Frontal plane
    B. Back of the heart
    C. Horizontal plane
    D. Vertical plane
4. As impulses travel through the heart, they generate small electrical forces called
    A. Electrical axis
    B. Bipolar lead

    C. Unipolar lead
    D. Instantaneous vectors
5. What is another word for electrical axis
    A. Instantaneous vectors
    B. Vertical axis
    C. Mean instantaneous vector
    D. Horizontal axis
6. In what position does the patient have to be during a ECG recording
    A. Prone position
    B. Supine position
    C. Lithotomy position
    D. Knee to chest position
7. During the bipolar limb lead, what acts as the ground lead
    A. Left arm
    B. Right leg
    C. Left leg
    D. Right arm
8. This records electrical activity in the heart's horizontal plane, providing a transverse view through the middle of the heart, dividing it into upper and lower portions
    A. Precordial leads
    B. 12-lead ECG
    C. Bipolar lead
    D. Unipolar lead

9. Where is lead V2 placed at
    A. Over fifth intercostal space at the left midaxillary line
    B. Over fourth intercostal space at the right sternal border
    C. Over fourth intercostal space at the left sternal border
    D. Over fifth intercostal space at the left midclavicular line
10. Where is lead V5 placed at
    A. Over fifth intercostal space at the left midclavicular line
    B. Over fourth intercostal space at the left sternal border
    C. Over fifth intercostal space at the left midaxillary line
    D. Over fifth intercostal space at left anterior axillary line
11. When all electrodes attached at one time to provide simultaneous view of all leads is called
    A. Signal- averaged ECG
    B. Precordial leads
    C. Bipolar leads
    D. Multichannel ECG
12. The use of computer to identify late electrical potentials from three specialized leads over hundreds of beat is called

    A. Monitor
    B. Signal averaged ECG
    C. Multichannel ECG
    D. Precordial leads
13. What is it called when a wave is upright, possibly inverted in lead aVr or biphasic or inverted in leads III, aVl, and V1
    A. P wave
    B. QRS complex
    C. PR interval
    D. ST segment
14. What type of wave shouldn't be tall, peaked, or notched
    A. P wave
    B. U wave
    C. T wave
    D. Q wave
15. This generally has a duration of less than 0.04 seconds
    A. T wave
    B. P wave
    C. Q wave
    D. U wave
16. What consists of six bisecting lines, each representing one of the six limb lead, and a circle, representing the heart
    A. Quadrant method

B. Hexaxial reference system
   C. Degree method
   D. R wave
17. This involves observing the main deflection of the QRS complex in leads I and aVf
    A. Degree method
    B. Hexaxial reference system
    C. R wave
    D. Quadrant method
18. What gives an exact degree measurement of the electrical axis
    A. Degree method
    B. Quadrant method
    C. 10 times method
    D. Sequence method
19. When the myocardium demands more oxygen than the coronary arteries can deliver is an episode of what
    A. Myocardium infarction
    B. Myocardium ischemia
    C. Angina
    D. Hypotension
20. When either the left or the right bundle branch fails to conduct impulses is called what
    A. Myocardium infarction
    B. Angina
    C. Bundle branch block

D. Bundle of his
21. The R wave represents what
    A. Atrial depolarization
    B. Late right ventricular depolarization
    C. Late left ventricular repolarization
    D. Late left ventricular depolarization
22. This usually occurs in the left ventricle, although the location may vary depending on the coronary artery affected
    A. Angina
    B. Myocardium ischemia
    C. Hypotension
    D. Myocardial infarction
23. This is caused by a blockage in the left circumflex artery and shows characteristic changes in the left lateral leads I, aVl, V5, and V6
    A. Lateral wall MI
    B. Septal wall MI
    C. Inferior wall MI
    D. Right ventricular MI
24. When the patient has an increased risk for developing a ventricular septal defect is called
    A. Lateral wall MI
    B. Inferior wall MI
    C. Right ventricular MI
    D. Septal wall MI

SECTION THREE ANSWERS

1. D
2. B
3. A
4. D
5. C
6. B
7. B
8. A
9. C
10. D
11. D
12. B
13. A
14. C
15. C
16. B
17. D
18. A
19. C
20. C
21. B
22. D
23. A
24. D

SECTION FOUR QUESTIONS

1. _____ point represents the exact point in time where ventricular depolarization stops and ventricular repolarization starts.

   A. F
   B. J
   C. G
   D. T

2. The Heart is how many chambered organ?

   A. Five
   B. Six
   C. Four
   D. Three

3. The heart circulates enough blood to deliver the much needed:

   A. Nitrogen.
   B. Oxygen.
   C. Calcium.
   D. Helium.

4. The _____ -lead EKG configuration is generally used to continuously monitor the patient's heart rhythm.

   A. 3
   B. 4

C. 5
D. 6

5. The heart wall is comprised of how many layers?

    A. Four layers.
    B. Two layers.
    C. Three layers.
    D. Five layers.

6. How many functional units do the septum separates the heart?

    A. Two.
    B. Five.
    C. Six.
    D. Three.

7. The mitral valve is situated between the:

    A. Right atrium and right ventricle.
    B. Left atrium and right ventricle.
    C. Right atrium and left atrium.
    D. Left atrium and left ventricle.

8. Deoxygenated blood is returned to the:

    A. Left atrium.

B. Right atrium.
C. Right ventricle.
D. Left ventricle.

9. The AV node serves as the primary pathway for impulses to travel from the
   Atria to the _____.

   A. Arteries.
   B. Ventricles.
   C. Pulmonary artery.
   D. All of the above.

10. In the absence of electrical stimulation from the SA and AV nodes, the _____ will fire at
    an intrinsic rate of 20 to 40/min.

    A. Bundle of His
    B. AV Node
    C. Purkinje fibers
    D. Internodal pathways

11. The _____ is a sophisticated tool that measures very low differences in electrical energy
    travelling across the surface of the human body.

    A. EEG

B. EKG
C. KKG
D. ELG

12. _____ is a reference point created by the three limb leads.

   A. Wilson's central terminal
   B. Einthoven's triangle
   C. J point
   D. Focal point

13. Standard EKG paper contains small boxes that measure ____ by____.

   A. 1m tall, 1mm wide
   B. 10mm tall, 1m wide
   C. 1mm tall, 10m wide
   D. 1mm tall, 1mm wide

14. Each millimeter increment on the y axis represents_____ millivolt.

   A. 0.01
   B. 0.1
   C. 1.0
   D. 10

15. Each millimeter increment on the X axis(horizontal) represents ____ milliseconds.

A. 0.4
B. 400
C. 40
D. 0.04

16. The standard paper speed is ____.
    A. 35mm/second
    B. 25mm/second
    C. 30mm/second
    D. 20mm/second

17. If Mike releases information about Mrs. Mary's diagnosis to her partner, which patient
    patient right has he violated.

    A. Patient confidentiality
    B. Negligence
    C. Refusal of care
    D. Patient consent

18. A lead that records the flow of electrical impulses between two electrodes of opposite polarity is called:

    A. Triploid.
    B. Unipolar.
    C. Bipolar.
    D. None of the above.

19. The triangle formed as a result of the axes of the three bipolar leads is
    called _____ triangle.

A. Beethoven's
B. Acute
C. Einthoven's
D. Scalene

20. The _____ represents the time it takes for the SA node to fire, atria to depolarize, and
    electricity to travel through the AV node.

   A. PR interval
   B. PR segment
   C. ST segment
   D. QRS complex

21. The distance from the onset of the QRS complex until the end of the T wave is
    Called.

   A. TQ interval.
   B. PT interval.
   C. QP interval.
   D. QT interval.

22. The QRS complex represents movement of the electrical impulses through
    the _____ causing their depolarization.

   A. Ventricles.

B. Atrium.
C. Kidney.
D. Lungs

23. . In lead V_1 the electrode is placed on right side of the sternum in the _____ intercostal space.

A. First
B. Third
C. Fourth
D. Second

24. How many seconds in duration represents each small square on the ECG papers that runs horizontally?

A. 0.4 seconds.
B. 0.20 seconds.
C. 0.12 seconds.
D. 0.04 seconds

25. Abnormalities in the cardiac rate and/or rhythm are called:

A. Pericardia.
B. Dysrhythmias.
C. Myocardial infarction.
D. None of the above.

26. The precordial V₁ electrode is placed on the _____ side of the sternum in
   fourth intercostal space.

   A. Left
   B. Middle
   C. Right
   D. All of the above.

27. Vertical markings on the top or bottom of the ECG paper represent _____
   intervals.

   A. 5 second
   B. 2 second
   C. 3 second
   D. 4 second

28. The point at which the QRS complex meets the ST segment is called the:

   A. QT point.
   B. J point.
   C. QS point.
   D. TS point.

29. . The precordial leads are obtained by placing electrodes on the patient's:

   A. Chest.
   B. Arms.

C. Legs.
D. Head.

30. The precordial leads are as follows:

    A. V1 and V2.
    B. I, II, and III.
    C. A and B
    D. V1, V2, V3, V4, V5, and V6.

31. The 6-second interval X 10 method involves multiplying 10 the number of QRS
    complexes found in a _____ portion of the ECG tracing.

    A. 4-second
    B. 5-second
    C. 6-second
    D. 3-second

32. The sequence method is also called _____.

    A. 6-second interval X 10 method.
    B. 1500 method.
    C. 3000, 150, 100, 60, 50 method
    D. 300, 150, 100, 75, 60, 50 method

33. The sequence method involves locating an R wave or a _____ on a bold line
    on the ECG paper.

A. T wave
B. P wave
C. Q wave
D. C wave

34. . When the heart rate is less than 60 beats per minute is called:

A. Cardiac arrest.
B. Bradycardia.
C. Tachycardia.
D. Heart Failure

35. A sinus bradycardia is a slow rate that arises from the:

A. Purkinje fibers
B. AV node
C. Aorta.
D. SA node

36. _____ is the complete cessation of electrical activity in the heart.

A. Asystole
B. Systole
C. Block
D. All of the above

37. Atrial flutter produces _____ atrial impulses per minute.

   A. 220 to 360
   B. 230 to 350
   C. 180 to 250
   D. 250 to 350

38. The 1500 method is named so because 1500 small squares on the ECG paper
   equal to _____

   A. One minute.
   B. Ten minute.
   C. Six minute.
   D. Two minute.

39. A heart rate greater than 100 is called:

   A. Myocardial infarction
   B. Tachycardia
   C. Bradycardia
   D. All of the above

40. Tachycardia that arises above the ventricles is called:

   A. Ventricular tachycardia
   B. Atrial fibrillation.
   C. Atrial flutter
   D. Supraventricular tachycardia

41. The heart rate for atrial tachycardia is generally between_____ beats.

   A. 160 to 250
   B. 180 to 350
   C. 150 to 250
   D. 100 to 180

42. . Atrial fibrillation produces greater than _____ atrial impulses per minute.

   A. 250 to 400
   B. 300 to 600
   C. 150 to 200
   D. 450 to 500

43. . An irregular rhythm is considered:

   A. Good
   B. Normal
   C. Abnormal
   D. Fast

44. To assess atrial regularity we analyze the _____ intervals.

   A. P-T
   B P-R
   C P-P
   D. R-R

45. . Consistently similar intervals represent a _____ rhythm

   A. Regular
   B. Irregular
   C. Fast
   D. Sporadic

46. An irregular rhythm can be caused by _____ complexes.

   A. Fast
   B. Slow
   C. Premature
   D. Mature

47. Electrical or magnetic interference that alters the EKG tracing is called:

   A. Art
   B. Artifact
   C. Disturbance
   D. Apex

48. The sensation of pain or discomfort in the chest is called:

   A. Ischemia
   B. Angina pectoris
   C. Cardiac arrest

D. Asystole

49. The lower pointed end of the heart is called:

    A. Apex
    B. Base
    C. Baseline
    D. A and B

50. A small muscular pouch-like structure that fills the ventricles with blood is called:
    A. Artery
    B. Valves
    C. Veins
    D. Atrium

51. P wave is the first waveform at the start of the____

    A. Cardiac level.
    B. Cardiac steps.
    C. Cardiac structure.
    D. Cardiac cycle.

52. Supraventricular tachycardia produces a heart rate of____ beats per minute.

    A. 120-150.
    B. 110-250.
    C. 150-240.
    D. 100-150.

53. Atrial fibrillation is associated with a:

   A. Characteristic flutters waveform.
   B. Characteristic P waveforms.
   C. Characteristic baseline form.
   D. Characteristic chaotic-looking baseline

54. Premature atrial complexes occur when?

   A. Electrical impulse travels through the atrial.
   B. Impulse arises from outside the AV junction.
   C. A site in the atria fires before the SA node is able to initiate an impulse
   D. All of the above

55. _____ are the not rhythms.

   A. PACs
   B. AVs
   C. SA
   D. All of the above

56. The QRS complex is the waveform immediately following the_____
   A. PS interval.
   B. PR interval.
   C. RS interval.
   D. QRS interval.

57. The duration of the normal QRS complex is:

   A. 0.06 to 0.20 seconds

B. 0.08 to 0.12 seconds
C. 0.02 to 0.15 seconds
D. 0.02 to 0.10 seconds

58. The first positive, triangular deflection in the QRS complex is:

    A. R wave
    B. Q wave
    C. S wave
    D. P wave

59. The first negative deflection that extends below the baseline in QRS complex is_____

    A. P wave
    B. R wave
    C. S wave
    D. Q wave

60. The point at which the QRS complex meet the ST segment is called?

    A. QRS junction
    B. J point
    C. T junction
    D. QRS point

61. Sinus bradycardia has a rate of less than____

    A. 60 beats per minute

B. 40 beat per minute
C. 80 beats per minute
D. 100 beats per minute

62. Junctional rhythm has a ventricular rate of____

   A. 20 to 50 beats per minute
   B. 40 to 60 beats per minute
   C. 20 to 60 beats per minute
   D. 10 to 40 beats per minute

63. Accelerated junctional rhythm has a QRS duration of _____ .

   A. 70 to 120 milliseconds
   B. 60 to 100 milliseconds
   C. 80 to 120 milliseconds
   D. 100 to 120 milliseconds

64. Ventricular tachycardia that arises from one site is called?

   A. Idioventricular
   B. Polymorphic
   C. Monomorphic
   D. PVC$_S$

65. . ____ is ventricular or cardiac standstill.

   A. Aberrant conduction
   B. Asystole

C. Ventricular fibrillation
D. QRS complex

66. Three or more PVCs in a row are considered____

   A. PVCs
   B. Ventricular dysrhythmias
   C. Ventricular tachycardia
   D. Idioventricular rhythm

67. The PR interval is the distance from the beginning of the P wave to:

   A. The end of the Q wave.
   B. The beginning of the PR wave.
   C. The end of the QRS waves.
   D. The beginning of the Q wave.

68. The duration of the normal PR intervals is:

   A. 0.20 to 0.30 seconds.
   B. 0.12 to 0.20 seconds.
   C. 0.4 to 0.15 seconds.
   D. 0.06 to 0.08 seconds.

69. PR intervals are considered abnormal if they are shorter than_____

   A. 0.11 seconds.
   B. 0.15 seconds.
   C. 0.12 seconds.
   D. 0.06 seconds.

70. PR intervals can also be considered abnormal if they are longer than____

    A. 0.30 seconds.
    B. 0.15 seconds.
    C. 0.08 seconds.
    D. 0.20 seconds.

71. ____ is the most common cause of longer than normal PR intervals.

    A. Wandering atrial pacemaker.
    B. Varying PR intervals.
    C. 2nd-degree AV heart block.
    D. 1st-degree AV heart block.

72. . In atrial flutter the atria fire at the rate of between____and____ beats per minute.

    A. 50 and 100.
    B. 240 and 320.
    C. 100 and 150
    D. 150 and 200

73. ____ is an ECG rhythm that differs from normal sinus rhythm.

    A. Ventricular.
    B. A dysrhythmia.
    C. Sinus arrest.
    D. Atrium.

74. . Rhythms originating from the SA node are called?

    A. Sinus rhythms.
    B. Sinus dysrhythmia.
    C. Sinus arrest.
    D. Sinus tachycardia.

75. Normal sinus rhythm is also referred to as:

    A. Irregular sinus rhythm.
    B. Regular sinus arrest.
    C. Regular sinus rhythm.
    D. Sinus dysrhythmia.

76. During normal heart activity, the SA node act as the_____

    A. Secondary pacemaker.
    B. Primary pacemaker.
    C. Atrial pacemaker.
    D. Ventricle pacemaker

77. Normal sinus rhythm has a heart rate of ___ to___ beats per minutes.

    A. 300, 500
    B. 20, 40
    C. 60, 100
    D. 150, 250

78. Sinus tachycardia is a faster than normal rhythm that results from:

   A. Decrease SA node stimulation and the heart rate.
   B. An increase in the rate of sinus node discharge.
   C. Increase in heart rate during inspiration and decrease during expiration.
   D. All of the above

79. The opposite of bradycardia is:

   A. Sinus.
   B. Dysrhythmia.
   C. Myocardial.
   D. Tachycardia.

80. In sinus tachycardia, the P waves, PR intervals, and QRS complexes are:

   A. Normal.
   B. Abnormal.
   C. Measurable.
   D. Flat.

81. _____ is a chronic disease characterize by thickening and hardening of the arteries.

   A. Cyanosis
   B. Arteriosclerosis

C. Pallor
D. None of the above

82. The act of opening a blood vessel is called:

A. Ectopic
B. Atherosclerosis
C. Vasodilation
D. Vasoconstriction

83. . Premature atrial complexes are early ectopic beats that originate outside the____

A. AV node.
B. AV junction.
C. PR interval.
D. SA node.

84. . When PACs are present, the first thing you see as you look across the ECG tracing is:

A. An irregular rhythm.
B. Normal rhythm.
C. Abnormal rhythm.
D. Regular rhythm.

85. Rhythms that originate in the AV junction, the area around the AV node and the bundle of His, are referred to as ___

A. Ventricular rhythm.
B. Atrial rhythm.

C. Junctional rhythms.
D. Dysrhythmias.

86. A _____ is a single early electrical impulse that originates in the AV junction.

    A. Supraventricular tachycardia.
    B. Atrial fibrillation.
    C. Premature junctional complex.
    D. Mature junctional complex.

87. _____ is dysrhythmia that arises from the AV junction.

    A. Junctional escape rhythm.
    B. Premature junctional complex.
    C. Accelerated junctional rhythm.
    D. Junctional tachycardia.

88. Accelerated junctional rhythm arises from above the _____, so the QRS complexes are normal.

    A. Atrial.
    B. P wave.
    C. SA node.
    D. Ventricles.

89. Polymorphic ventricular Tachycardia has a ventricular rate greater than_____

    A. 100/min
    B. 130/min

C. 120/min
D. 140/min

90. _____ is a rhythm in which the pacemaker site shifts between the SA node, atria, and AV junction.

    A. Atrial kick.
    B. Wandering atrial pacemaker.
    C. Wandering ventricular pacemaker.
    D. Premature atrial complex.

91. One of the first things you see with a PVC is an _____ rhythm.

    A. Irregular.
    B. Regular.
    C. Abnormal.
    D. Normal.

92. Like PACs, _____ are not rhythms.
    A. PVCs
    B. PVAs
    C. PCAs
    D. PRs

93. PVCs that look the same are called?

    A. Intermingle.
    B. Uniform.
    C. Multiform
    D. Double-look.

94. Which of the following AV heart blocks is considered a consistent delay of conduction at the level of the AV node?

    A. 1st-degree AV heart block.
    B. 2nd-degree AV heart block, Type I.
    C. 2nd-degree AV heart block, Type II.
    D. 3rd-degree AV heart block.

95. The most obvious characteristic of the 1st-degree is PR intervals greater than ___ seconds in duration and constant.

    A. 0.50
    B. 0.10
    C. 0.15
    D. 0.20

96. Questions about social history include the following except:

    A. Determine the patient's marital status and whether he/she has children
    B. What does the patient east?
    C. Ask a female patient if she is pregnant
    D. Does the patient drink alcohol or use drugs?

97. What AV heart block is an intermittent block at the level of the AV node?

    A. 1st-degree AV heart block.

B. 2nd-degree AV heart block, Type I.
C. 2nd-degree AV heart block, Type II.
D. 3rd-degree AV heart block.

98. Wenckebach is another name for __

   A. 1st-degree AV heart block.
   B. 2nd-degree AV heart block, Type II.
   C. 2nd-degree AV heart block, Type I.
   D. 3rd-degree AV heart block.

99. 3rd-degree AV heart block is a:

   A. Complete block of the conduction at or below the AV node.
   B. Intermittent block at the level of the bundle of His.
   C. Intermittent block at the level of the AV node.
   D. Consistent delay of conduction at the level of the AV node.

100. In 3rd-degree AV heart block, SA node serves as the pacemaker for the atria, typically maintaining a regular rate of __ to __ beats per minute.

   A. 20 to 50
   B. 10 t0 30
   C. 60 to 100
   D. 100 to 150

EKG
ANSWERS
1. B
2. C
3. B
4. A
5. C
6. A
7. D
8. B
9. B
10. C
11. B
12. B

13. D
14. B
15. D
16. B
17. A
18. C
19. C
20. A
21. D
22. A
23. C
24. D
25. B
26. C
27. C
28. B
29. A
30. D
31. C
32. D
33. B
34. B
35. D
36. A
37. D
38. A
39. B
40. D
41. A
42. B
43. C

44. C
45. A
46. C
47. B
48. B
49. A
50. D
51. D
52. C
53. D
54. C
55. A
56. B
57. B
58. A
59. C
60. B
61. A
62. B
63. C
64. C
65. B
66. C
67. D
68. B
69. C
70. D
71. D
72. B
73. B
74. A

75. C
76. B
77. C
78. B
79. D
80. C
81. B
82. C
83. D
84. A
85. C
86. C
87. C
88. A
89. C
90. B
91. A
92. A
93. B
94. A
95. D
96. A
97. B
98. C
99. A
100.

SECTION FIVE QUESTIONS

1. The electrocardiogram, often referred to as an ECG or EKG, is a tracing or graphic representation of the heart's :

    A. Electrical volts.
    B. Electrical energy
    C. Electrical activity
    D. Electrical pulse.

2. The EKG is used to Identify irregularities in the heart:

    A. Beats.
    B. Pulse
    C. Movements.
    D. Rhythm.

3. Impulses that move toward a positive electrode of the ECG produce a:

    A. Negative.
    B. Positive.
    C. Neutral
    D. None of the above.

4. Which organ is the pump of the circulatory system?

    A. The kidney.

87

B. The lungs
C. The heart
D. The liver.

5. The heart circulates enough blood to deliver the much needed:
A. Nitrogen.
B. Oxygen.
C. Calcium.
D. Helium.

6. Pericardium is also known as:

A. Scrotal sac.
B. Pericardial sac.
C. Bradycardia.
D. Tachycardia.

7. The cell in the heart which contracts to propel blood out of it's
Chambers is called:

A. Myocardial cells.
B. Living cells.
C. Rotating cells.
D. Red blood cells.

8. Which of the following permit the rapid conduction of electrical impulses
from one cell to another?

A. Tap junctions.
B. Intercalated disks.
C. Syncytium.
D. Gap junction.

9. The heart wall is comprised of how many layers?

A. Four layers.
B. Two layers.
C. Three layers.
D. Five layers.

10. The heart is shaped like a:

A. Triangle
B. Sharp cone.
C. Blunt cone.
D. None of the above.

11. The inner, thin, transparent lining of the pericardium is called?

A. Serous pericardium.
B. Fibrous pericardium.
C. Cancerous pericardium.
D. Inner heart membrane.

12. The myocytes are cylindrical and branching at their:

A. Middle disks.

B. Beginning disks.
C. Centre disks.
D. End disks.

13. The heart is referred to as a:

    A. Single pump.
    B. Double pump.
    C. Triple pump.
    D. None of the above.

14. How many functional units do the septum separates the heart?

    E. Two.
    F. Five.
    G. Six.
    H. Three.

15. The mitral valve is situated between the:

    E. Right atrium and right ventricle.
    F. Left atrium and right ventricle.
    G. Right atrium and left atrium.
    H. Left atrium and left ventricle.

16. How many cusps do the tricuspid valve has?

    A. Three.

B. Two.
C. Five.
D. No cusps.

17. The pulmonic valve is located at the base of:

   A. Aorta.
   B. Brachial artery.
   C. Pulmonary artery.
   D. Popliteal artery.

18. Due to how the cardiac muscles are attached and arranged, the ventricles
   Contract with a _____ motion.

   A. Rapid motion.
   B. Wringing motion.
   C. Jumping motion.
   D. Leaping motion.

19. The skeleton of the heart provides support for the:

   A. Pulmonary artery.
   B. Coronary artery.
   C. Axial artery.
   D. Atrioventricular.

20. The heart receives most of its blood supply through the:

    A. Coronary arteries.
    B. Brachial arteries.
    C. Pulmonary arteries.
    D. All of the above.

21. Which nervous system helps regulate the rate and strength of the myocardial contractions?

    A. Automatic nervous system.
    B. Manual nervous system.
    C. Autonomic nervous system.
    D. Semi-automatic nervous system.

22. Deoxygenated blood is returned to the:

    E. Left atrium.
    F. Right atrium.
    G. Right ventricle.
    H. Left ventricle.

23. How many phases of the cardiac cycle exists?

    A. Three phases.
    B. Five phases.
    C. Four phases.
    D. Two phases.

24. The contraction of the atria and ventricles is referred as:

A. Systole.
B. Diastole.
C. Manostole.
D. All of the above.

25. The amount of blood ejected from the ventricles is referred as:

    A. High volume.
    B. Stroke volume.
    C. Stress volume.
    D. Low volume.

26. Cardiac output is the amount of blood pumped out from the heart in:

    A. Four minutes.
    B. Six minutes.
    C. One minute.
    D. Ten minutes.

27. Chemoreceptors have the job of sensing changes in the_____
    Composition of the blood.

    A. Physical.
    B. Mental.
    C. Structural.
    D. Chemical.

28. Which cells in the heart can generate electrical impulses on their own?

   A. Myocardial cells.
   B. Bradycardia cells.
   C. Tachycardia cells.
   D. All of the above.

29. At which state is the inside of the myocardial cells more negatively charged
      relative to outside of the cells.

   A. Polaroid.
   B. Polarized.
   C. Regularized state.
   D. None of the above.

30. The blood is pumped through systemic circulation to deliver_____
      to the tissues.

   A. Carbon dioxide.
   B. Hydrogen.
   C. Nitrogen.
   D. Oxygen.

31. Bicuspid valve is also known as:

   A. Liter valve.
   B. Lateral valve.
   C. Mitral valve.

D. Tricuspid valve.

32. The AV node serves as the primary pathway for impulses to travel from the
   Atria to the _____.

   E. Arteries.
   F. Ventricles.
   G. Pulmonary artery.
   H. All of the above.

33. The impulse is slowed down as it passes from the atria to the ventricles
   Through the:

   A. AV node.
   B. AZ node.
   C. SA node.
   D. None of the above.

34. Sodium, calcium and _____ are the key electrolytes responsible for
   Initiating electrical activity.

   A. Magnesium.
   B. Helium.
   C. Oxygen.
   D. Potassium.

35. The right and left bundles terminate in the:

    A. Optic fibers.
    B. Neurotic fibers.
    C. Purkinje fibers.
    D. Automatic fibers.

36. The ability of certain myocardial cells to produce electrical activity
Without the need for outside nerve stimulation is called:

    A. Excitability.
    B. Conductivity.
    C. Automaticity.
    D. Contractility.

37. Parasympathetic stimulation causes _____ of the heart rate and AV
Conduction.

    A. Stopping.
    B. Slowing.
    C. Fastening.
    D. Moving.

38. _____ is the ability to respond to an electrical stimulus.

    A. Excitability.
    B. Conductivity.
    C. Automaticity.
    D. Flexibility.

39. Effects produced by the sympathetic nervous system includes increased
Heart rate and _____ contractility.

   A. Decreased.
   B. Improved.
   C. Reduced.
   D. Increased.

40. The heart is primarily stimulated by:

   A. Alpha receptors.
   B. Gamma receptors.
   C. Fiber receptors.
   D. Beta receptors.

41. The average heart rate in the adult is:

   A. 82 beats per minute.
   B. 75 beats per minute.
   C. 52 beats per minute.
   D. 92 beats per minute.

42. Which of the pacemaker sites is the primary pacemaker?

   A. AM node.
   B. AV node.
   C. SA node.
   D. SV node.

43. The intrinsic rate of the AV node is:

A. 40 to 60 beats per minute.
B. 50 to 70 beats per minute.
C. 60 to 80 beats per minute.
D. 50 to 50 beats per minute.

44. The intrinsic rate of the SA node is:

A. 60 to 80 beats per minute.
B. 80 to 100 beats per minute.
C. 50 to 110 beats per minute.
D. 60 to 100 beats per minute.

45. The ventricular repolarization is represented by the:

A. Q wave.
B. H wave.
C. T wave.
D. L wave.

46. The average liter of blood pumped by the heart in a day is:

A. 3000 and 5000 liters.
B. 6000 and 8000 liters.
C. 6000 and 9000 liters.
D. 7000 and 9000 liters.

47. The specialized structures in the cellular membrane which hold the
    myocytes together to prevent them from pulling apart when the heart
    contracts is:

    A. Chromosomes.
    B. Hormones.
    C. Desmosomes.
    D. DNA.

48. The nervous control of the heart originates from two separate nerve centers
    Located in the:

    A. Cerebellum.
    B. Medulla oblongata.
    C. Hypothalamus.
    D. Mid brain.

49. Nerve impulses stimulate muscles cells to:

    A. Contract.
    B. Conduct.
    C. Expand.
    D. All of the above.

50. The lower chambers of the heart are called the:

    A. Ventricles.
    B. Atria

C. Venules.
D. Vena cava.

SECTION FIVE ANSWERS.

1. C
2. D
3. B
4. C
5. B
6. B
7. A
8. D
9. C
10. C
11. A
12. D
13. B
14. A
15. D
16. A
17. C
18. B
19. D
20. A
21. C
22. B
23. D
24. A
25. B
26. C
27. D
28. A

29. B
30. D
31. C
32. B
33. A
34. D
35. C
36. C
37. B
38. A
39. D
40. D
41. B
42. C
43. A
44. D
45. C
46. D
47. C
48. B
49. A
50. A

SECTION SIX QUESTIONS

1. The hearts electrical activity is detected by the _____ positioned on the patients skin.

    A. Cathodes.
    B. Electrodes.
    C. Anodes.
    D. None of the above.

2. What transfers electrical activity back to the ECG machine were it can be displayed on the oscilloscope?

    A. Copper wires.
    B. Aluminum wires.
    C. Lead wires.
    D. Titanium wires.

3. The paper, made of thermally sensitive material, consists of _____ and _____ lines that form a grid.

    A. Horizontal, vertical.
    B. Parallel, horizontal.
    C. Vertical, circled.
    D. All of the above.

4. When no electrical stimulus is flowing through the electrode, or it is too small to detect, the stylus burns a_____ line.

A. Circled.
   B. Curved.
   C. Squared.
   D. Straight.

5. The distance between the lines, or boxes, running horizontally represents :
   A. Space.
   B. Amplitude.
   C. Time.
   D. Voltage.

6. The flat line shown when no electrical activity is occurring or it is too weak to be detected is called:

   A. Bioelectric line.
   B. Symmetric line.
   C. Electric line.
   D. Isoelectric line.

7. The initiation of the impulse in the SA node and its movement through the atria produces a:

   A. T wave.
   B. P wave.
   C. C wave.
   D. Q wave.

8. The _____ interval is the distance from the beginning of the P wave to the beginning of the Q wave.

   A. PR interval.
   B. QR interval.
   C. TR interval.
   D. RS interval.

9. Following the PR segment we should see a _____ complex.

   A. QRS complex.
   B. QRX complex.
   C. QSR complex
   D. QXS complex.

10. The R wave is the first upward deflection after the:

    A. S wave.
    B. T wave.
    C. P wave.
    D. Q wave.

11. A lead that records the flow of electrical impulses between two electrodes of opposite polarity is called:

    E. Bipolar.
    F. Unipolar.
    G. Triploid.

H. None of the above.

12. The triangle formed as a result of the axes of the three bipolar leads is
called _____ triangle.

    D. Beethoven's
    E. Acute
    F. Einthoven's
    G. Scalene.

13. Bipolar leads have a third electrode called a:

    A. Land.
    B. Sand.
    C. Ground.
    D. Down.

14. A lead that uses one positive electrode and a reference is called:

    A. Unipolar.
    B. Bipolar.
    C. Single Polar.
    D. All of the above.

15. The limb leads view the _____ .

    A. Horizontal plane.
    B. Frontal plane.
    C. Back plane.

D. Side plane.

16. The precordial leads view the heart's electrical activity on the _____ .

    A. Frontal plane.
    B. Side plane.
    C. Horizontal plane.
    D. None of the above.

17. Markings on the ECG tracing that are not a product of the electrical activity
    Of the heart are called:

    A. Isoelectric.
    B. Flat line.
    C. Bioelectric.
    D. Artifact.

18. After the QRS complex, we should see a flat line referred to as the_____
    Segment.

    A. TS.
    B. ST.
    C. T.
    D. S.

19. The distance from the onset of the QRS complex until the end of the T wave is Called......................

    A. TQ interval.

B. PT interval.
C. QP interval.
D. QT interval.

20. The QRS complex represents movement of the electrical impulses through the _____ causing their contraction.

    A. Ventricles.
    B. Atrium.
    C. Kidney.
    D. Lungs.

21. Which wave is not always present?

    A. T wave.
    B. P wave.
    C. Q wave.
    D. R wave.

22. A normal PR interval is _____ seconds:

    A. 0.14 to 0.16
    B. 0.12 to 0.20
    C. 0.13 to 0.20
    D. 0.12 to 0.16

23. The QT interval has a normal duration of:

    A. 0.30 to 0.44 seconds.
    B. 0.26 to 0.44 seconds.
    C. 0.36 to 0.56 seconds.

D. 0.36 to 0.44 seconds.

24. The _____ leads are obtained by placing electrodes on the patient's extremities.

   A. Limb.
   B. Precordial.
   C. Rear.
   D. Hind.

25. With lead II the _____ electrode is placed on the left leg or on the left midclavicular line, below the last palpable rib.

   A. Neutral
   B. Negative
   C. Ground
   D. Positive.

26. Which lead is commonly used for continuous ECG monitoring?

   A. Lead I
   B. Lead II
   C. Lead III
   D. Lead IV.

27. The precordial leads are also called:

   A. T leads

B. V leads
C. S leads
D. Q leads

28. In lead V_1 the electrode is placed on right side of the sternum in the _____ intercostal space.

A. First
B. Third
C. Fourth
D. Second

29. Electrical currents travelling toward a positive electrode produce a waveform that takes an/a _____ deflection.

A. Upright
B. Downward
C. Backward
D. All of the above.

30. _____ presents a view of the heart's electrical activity between one positive Pole and one negative pole.

A. Plane
B. Section
C. Lead
D. None of the above.

31. Planes provide a _____ view of the heart.

A. Cross-sectional.
B. Parallel
C. Adjacent
D. Horizontal

32. The direction the electrical impulse takes toward or away from a positive electrode causes the waveform to deflect either _____ or _____.

A. Upward or Forward
B. Downward or Backward
C. Downward or upward
D. Upward or downward

33. The 12-lead ECG provides a more complete picture of the heart's electrical activity; it provides _____ views.

A. 4
B. 12
C. 6
D. 3

34. Lead V_5 is positioned at the fifth intercostal space at the anterior _____ line.

A. Midaxillary
B. Midcalvicular
C. Axillary

D. None of the above.

35. With MCL$_1$, the positive electrode is positioned in the _____ intercostal
Space in the right sternal border.

   A. Second
   B. Fourth
   C. Fifth
   D. Third

36. ECG rhythms shown on the oscilloscope are called _____ ECGs

   A. Dynamic
   B. Static
   C. Steady
   D. All of the above.

37. How many seconds in duration represents each small square on the ECG
papers that runs horizontally?

   A. 0.4 seconds.
   B. 0.20 seconds.
   C. 0.12 seconds.
   D. 0.04 seconds

38. Abnormalities in the cardiac rate and/or rhythm are called:

   A. Pericardia.

B. Dysrhythmias.
C. Myocardial infarction.
D. None of the above.

39. The precordial V_1 electrode is placed on the _____ side of the sternum in fourth intercostal space.

A. Left
B. Middle
C. Right
D. All of the above.

40. With MCL_6, the positive lead is placed at the _____ intercostal space at the midaxillary line.

A. First
B. Second
C. Fourth
D. Fifth

41. In lead aV_F the positive electrode is located on the:

A. Left arm.
B. Right arm.
C. Both arms.
D. Legs

42. The standard limb leads are which leads?

A. V_1, V_2, V_3, V_4, V_5, and V_6.
B. MCL_1 and MCL_2.
C. I, II, and III.
D. All of the above.

43. Vertical markings on ECG paper represent _____

    A. Seconds
    B. Duration
    C. Millivolts
    D. A and B

44. The point at which the QRS complex meets the ST segment is called the:

    A. QT point.
    B. J point.
    C. QS point.
    D. TS point.

45. The precordial leads are obtained by placing electrodes on the patient's:

    A. Chest.
    B. Arms.
    C. Legs.
    D. Head.

46. _____ nerves controls the heart rate.

A. Diaphragmatic
B. Vagus
C. Aortic
D. Purkinje

47. The precordial leads are as follows:

   A. MCL1 and MCL2.
   B. I, II, and III.
   C. A and B
   D. V1, V2, V3, V4, V5, and V6.

48. What seconds in duration, is the larger box made up of five small squares,
    represents on the ECG paper?

   A. 0.12
   B. 0.15
   C. 0.20
   D. 0.32

49. The _____ is the first deflection after the PR segment.

   A. T wave
   B. Q wave
   C. P wave
   D A and C

50. Sixty large boxes on the ECG paper represent :

A. 6 seconds
B. 8 seconds
C. 12 seconds
D. 18 seconds.

SECTION SIX ANSWERS.

1. B
2. C
3. A
4. D
5. C
6. D
7. B
8. A
9. A
10. D
11. A
12. C
13. C
14. A
15. B
16. C
17. D
18. B
19. D
20. A
21. C
22. B
23. D
24. A
25. D
26. B
27. B
28. C

29. A
30. C
31. A
32. D
33. B
34. C
35. B
36. A
37. D
38. B
39. C
40. D
41. A
42. C
43. D
44. B
45. A
46. B
47. D
48. C
49. B
50. C

GOOD LUCK IN YOUR EXAMS!!!

Made in the USA
San Bernardino, CA
03 August 2017